BIOGRAPHIES FOR KIDS

All about Rosa Parks:
The Civil Rights Movement of America

Children's Biographies of Famous People Books

BABY PROFESSOR

EDUCATION KIDS

Speedy Publishing LLC

40 E. Main St. #1156

Newark, DE 19711

www.speedypublishing.com

Copyright 2015

WHO IS ROSA PARKS?

WHAT DID SHE DO TO INFLUENCE THE AMERICAN CIVIL RIGHTS MOVEMENT?

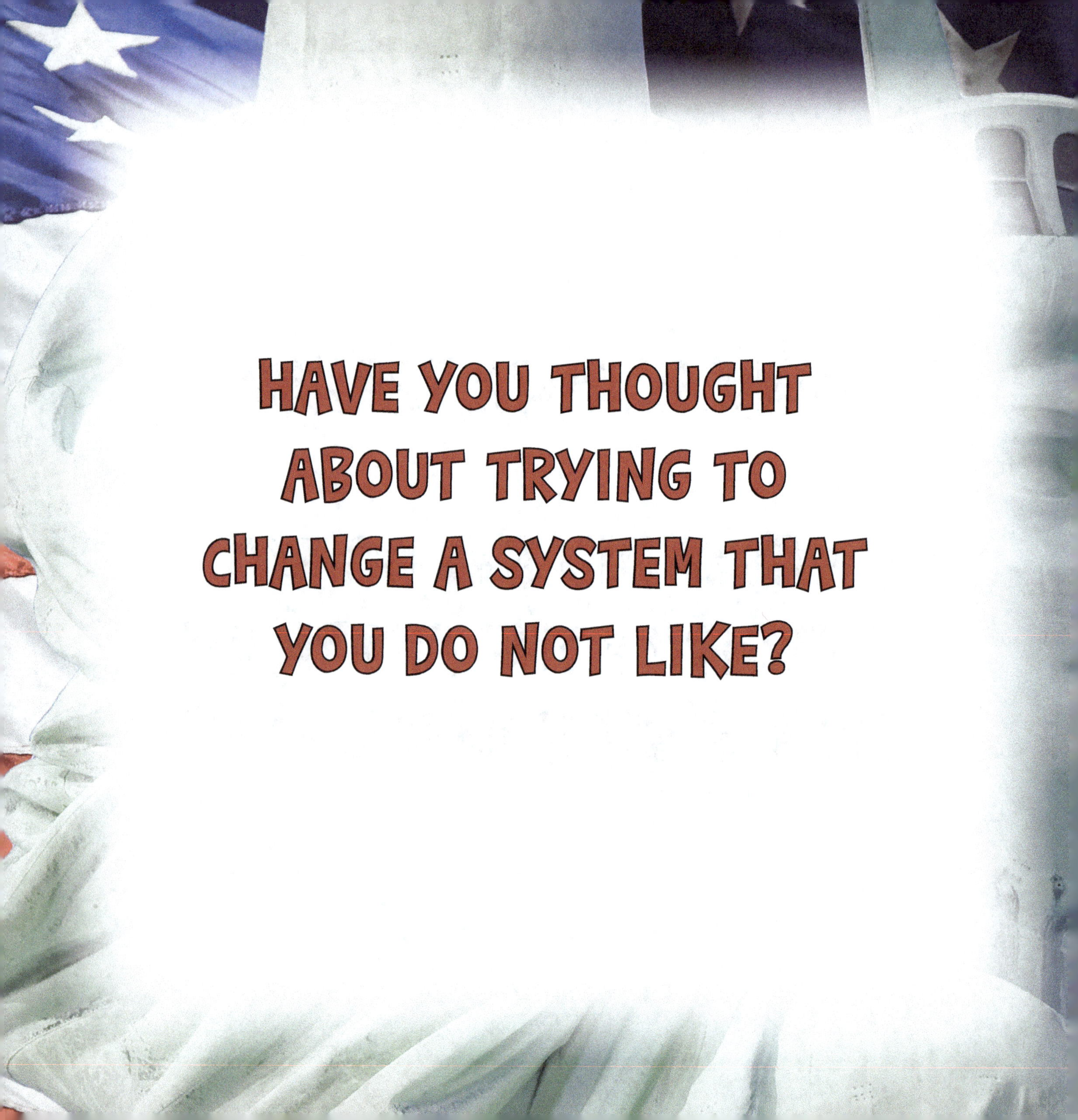

HAVE YOU THOUGHT ABOUT TRYING TO CHANGE A SYSTEM THAT YOU DO NOT LIKE?

WHAT QUALITIES SHOULD YOU HAVE TO IMPLEMENT GREAT CHANGE IN THE COMMUNITY?

HANDS UP DON'T SHOO
BLACK LIVES MATTER

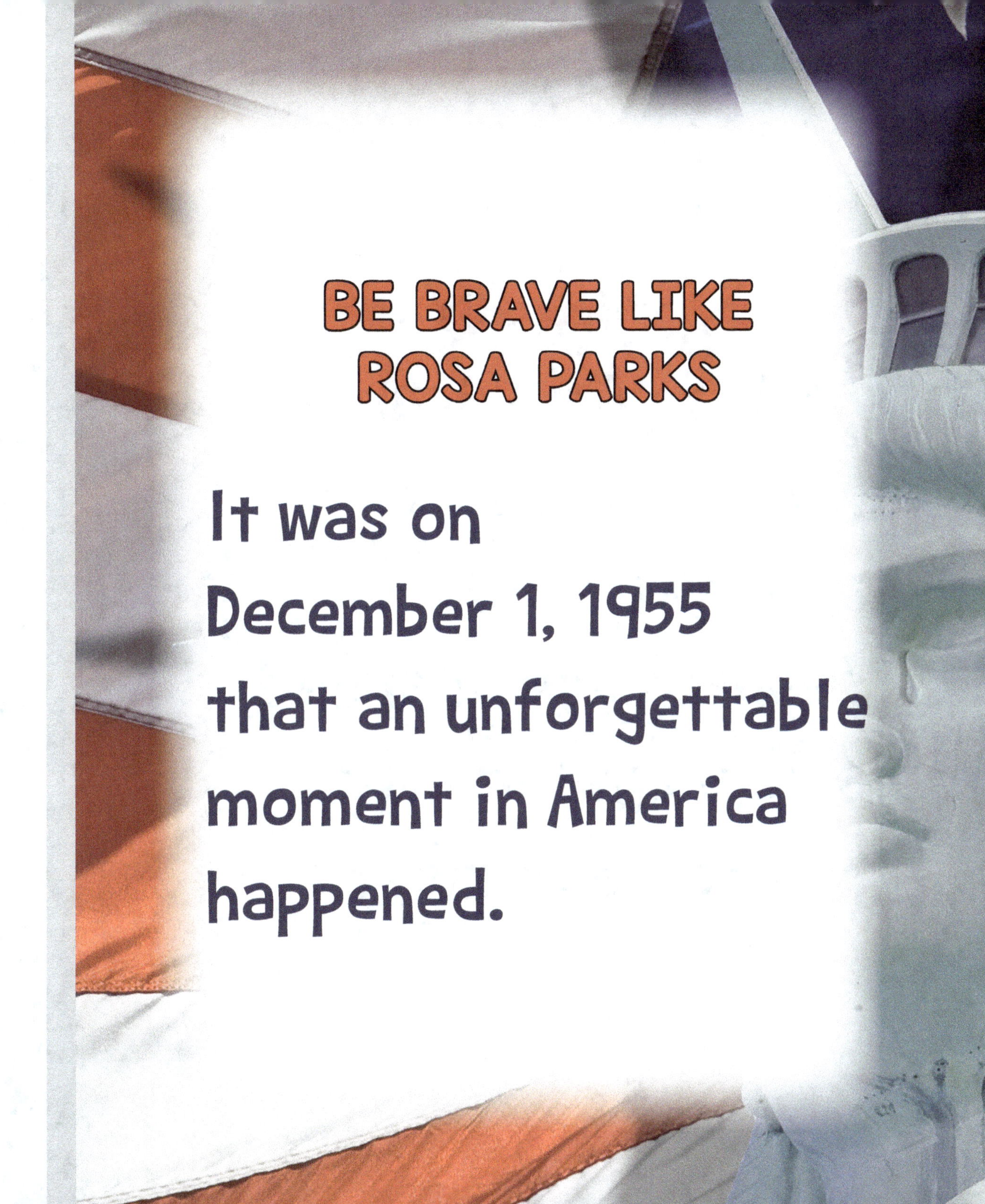

BE BRAVE LIKE ROSA PARKS

It was on December 1, 1955 that an unforgettable moment in America happened.

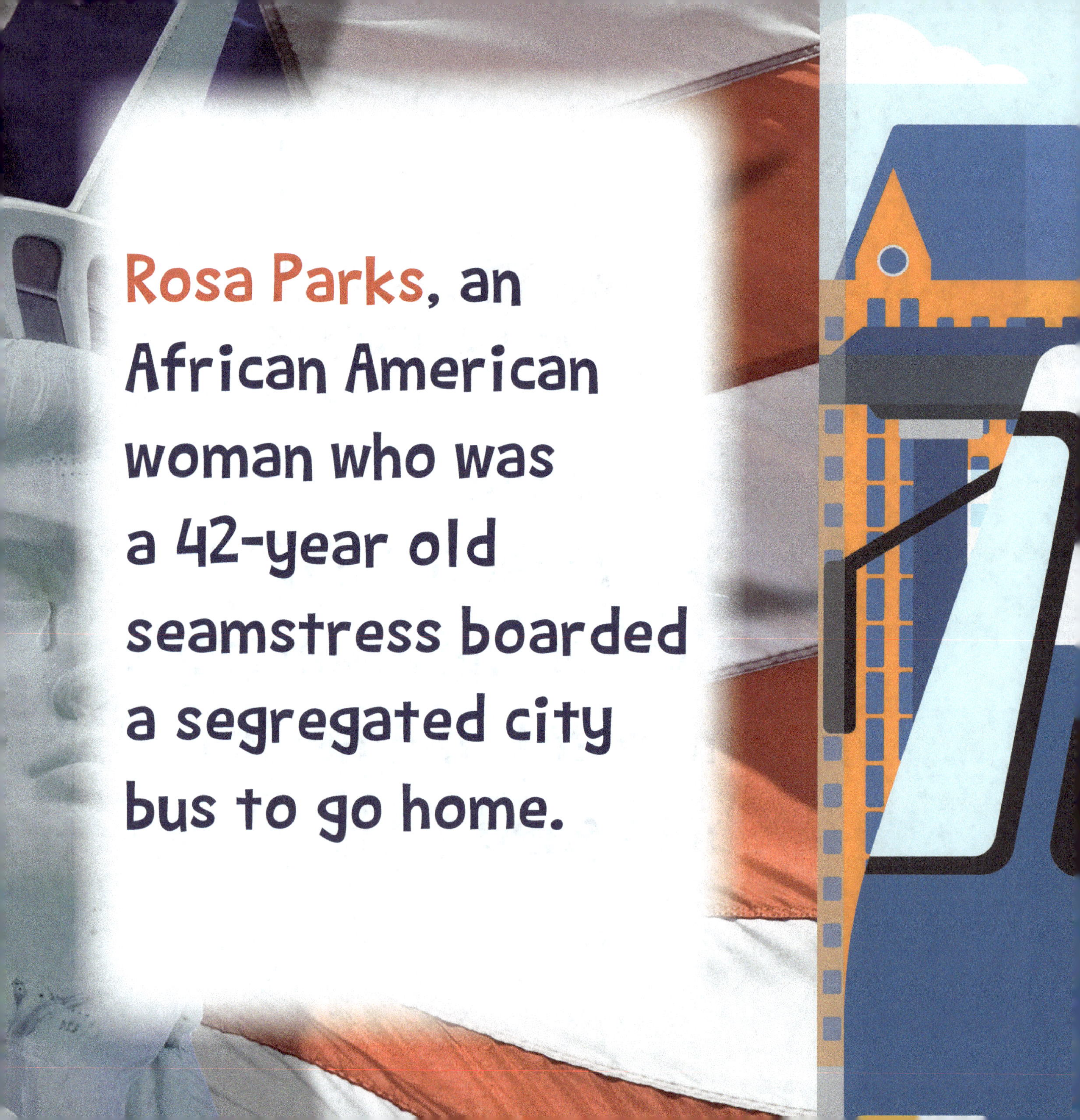

Rosa Parks, an African American woman who was a 42-year old seamstress boarded a segregated city bus to go home.

She refused to give up her seat to a White man when the bus became full.

She was ordered by the bus
driver to give her seat.
But Rosa firmly refused
to do so and stayed in her
seat.

Civil Rights

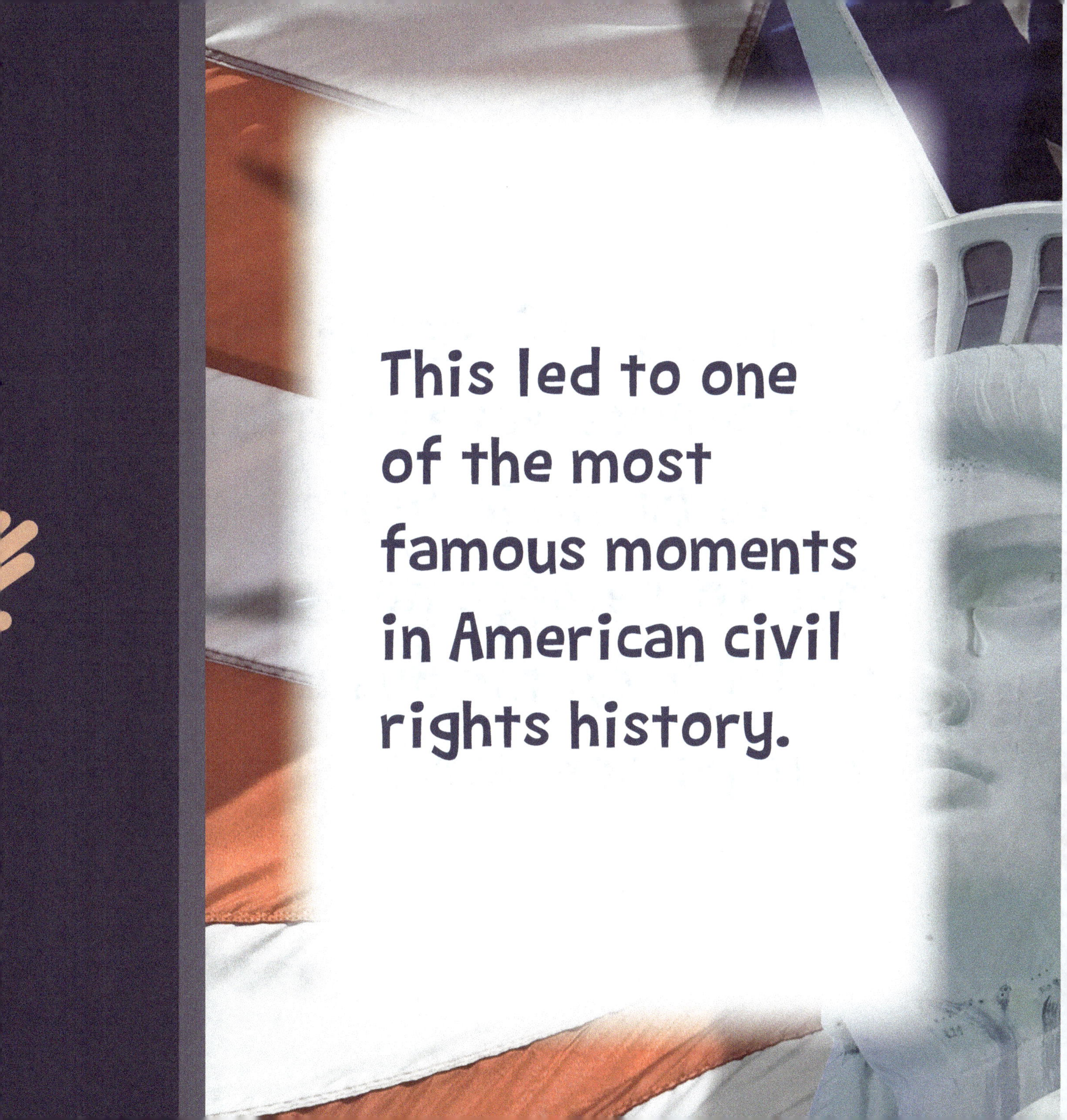

This led to one of the most famous moments in American civil rights history.

According to Segregation laws, blacks were mandated to give up their seats when there were no seats available on the bus and a white person got on the bus,

So by not giving up her seat, Rosa Parks defied the norms of the society where she lived.

Breaking the
existing laws
of segregation
required great
strength and
courage which lead
to her arrest.

RACE
SCRIMINATION

MR. PRESIDENT
HOW LONG
MUST
WOMEN WAIT
FOR LIBERTY

Rosa Parks and her flawless reputation defined the modern American Civil Rights Movement.

Rosa Park's meaningful act sparked a social transformation.

ight makes
might

This somewhat changed the racial relations in America. But it was noted that there were other black women who fought back before Rosa Parks.

These were Susie McDonald, Aurelia Browder, Mary Louise Smith and Claudette Colvin. All of them were allegedly arrested on buses in Montgomery for challenging the law.

But Rosa Park's defiance
of the segregation law
was seen as different and
unique. Her arrest brought
the community to act and
respond.

Her innate personality brought this climactic change in American civil rights history.

ALL VETERANS UNITE
IN THE DRIVE
FOR THE BONUS
WE DEMAND THE
BONUS
for
ALL Veterans

Her flawless character, inner strength and fortitude inspired the boycott of black people using the public buses in Montgomery which lasted 381 days.

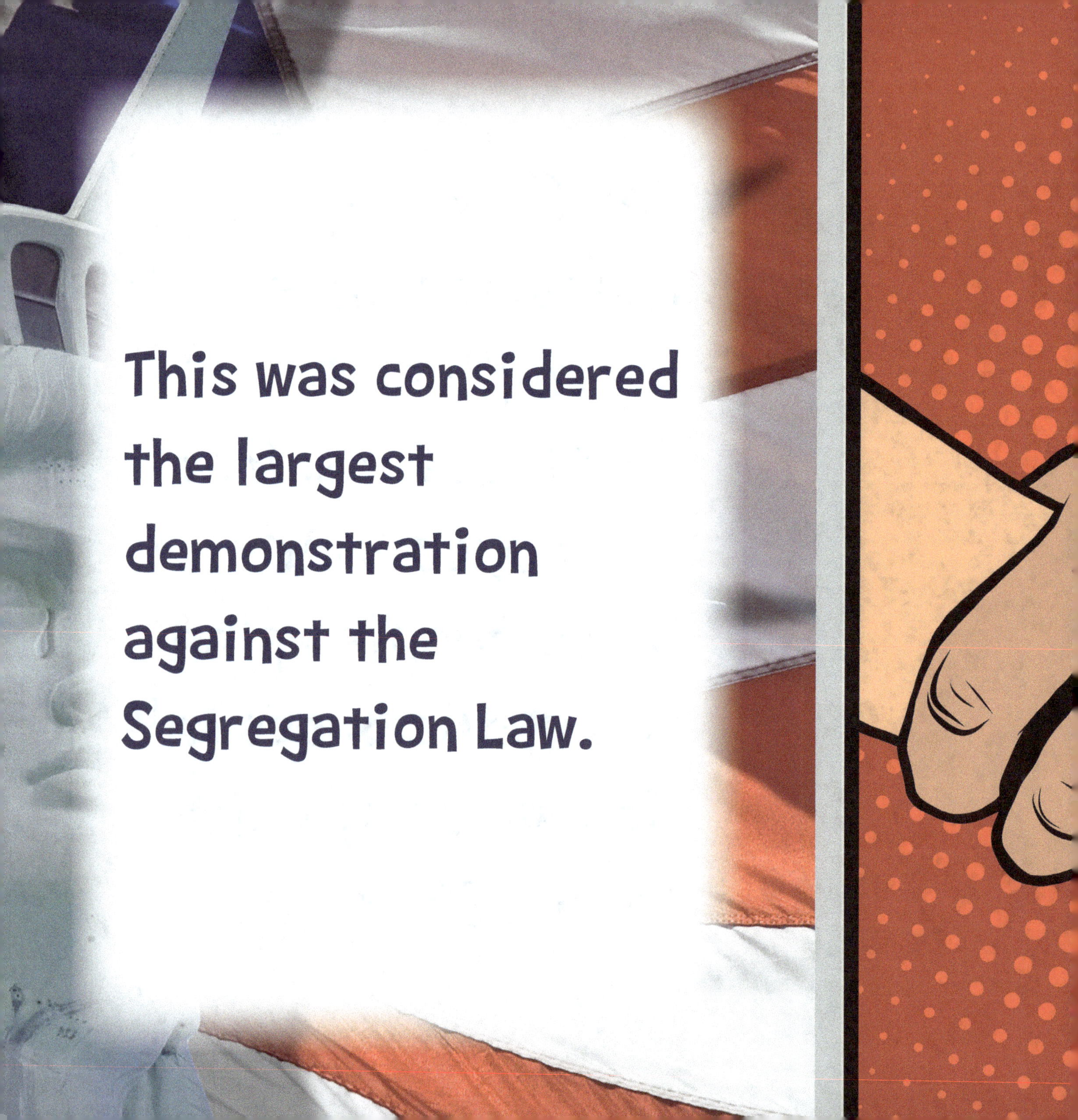

This was considered the largest demonstration against the Segregation Law.

As a result, the boycott made the US Supreme Court to recall the segregation law on public buses in Alabama.

Moreover, nonviolent protests became evident in many other cities. Then Martin Luther King Jr., a young Baptist minister became the leader of the civil rights movement.

Civil
Rights

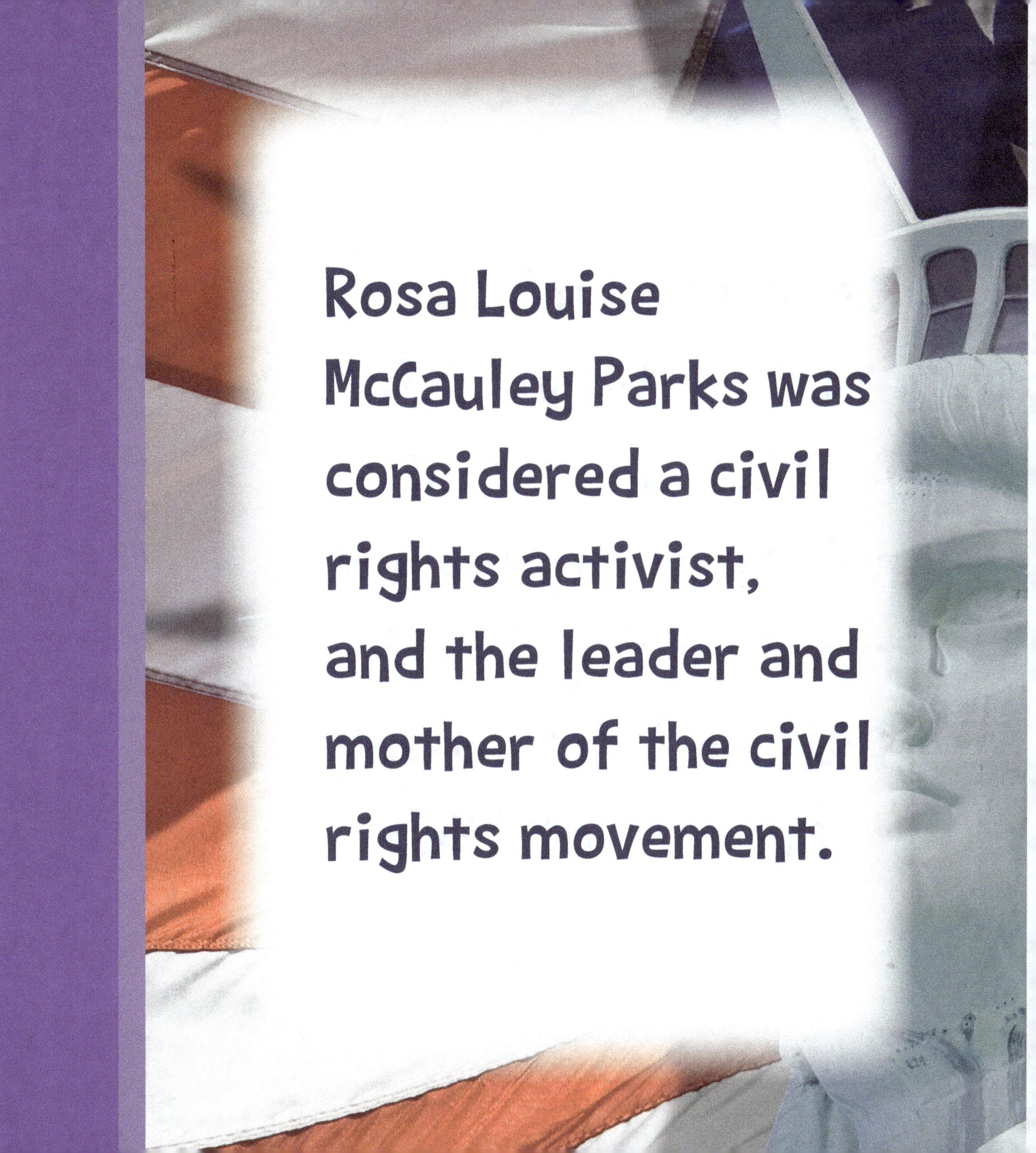
Rosa Louise McCauley Parks was considered a civil rights activist, and the leader and mother of the civil rights movement.

Her meaningful
act to achieve fair
justice and racial
relations prompted
the Civil Rights of
1964 and the Voting
Rights Act of 1965.

CIVIL
RIGHTS

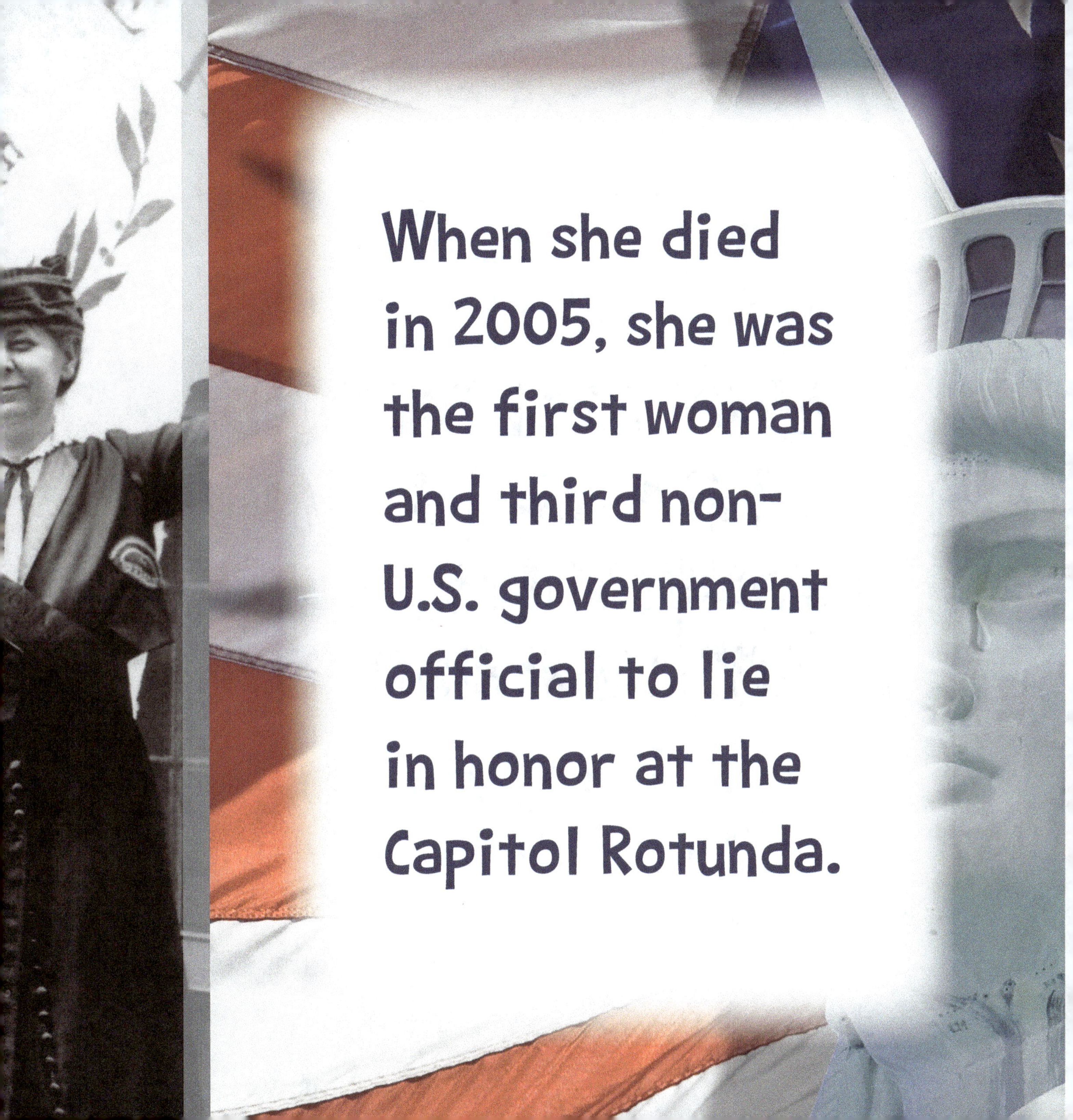
When she died
in 2005, she was
the first woman
and third non-
U.S. government
official to lie
in honor at the
Capitol Rotunda.

WHAT ROSA PARK DID
WAS A HUGE SOCIAL
REVOLUTION IN MODERN
AMERICAN HISTORY.

DO YOU KNOW SOMEONE
AS BRAVE AS ROSA PARK?

Visit
BABY PROFESSOR
EDUCATION KIDS
www.BabyProfessorBooks.com
to download Free Baby Professor eBooks
and view our catalog of new and exciting
Children's Books